HALF A MO!

A COLLECTION OF STORIES AND RHYMES

BY

MAURICE A. STURGEON.

ILLUSTRATIONS BY ANDREA CAHILL.

PUBLISHED BY BIRDS HILL PUBLICATIONS.

PRINTED BY THE CATFORD PRESS.

Published by:
Birds Hill Publications,
24 Goldfinch Close, Birds Hill, Chelsfield, Kent BR6 6NF
Telephone and Fax: 01689 850859

ISBN 1 900894 00 9.

Printed by:
The Catford Press, 3 Bellingham Road, Catford, London SE6 2PN

CONTENTS.

INTRODUCTION.

There were many ways to set out this anthology, but as far as possible I have arranged the contents to correspond with the different phases of my journey through time.

The anecdotes and accounts relate to true events. The poems were mostly written to amuse, provoke and occasionally infuriate my family and friends.

The "Hospice Visitor" was composed, perhaps inspired, as a result of my lifelong interest in matters spiritual and the mystery of other dimensions.

My sincere thanks to Andrea, the illustrator, for her patience and good humour.

My gratitude to the "Granville Writers" - without their continual encouragement, this work might never have materialised.

With love to my family, I dedicate this book to my four grandchildren,

THOMAS, JOSEPH, LAURA AND JOSHUA.

May they enjoy tomorrow.

TIME.

Can you remember as a child
Awaiting for some great event
And how the time would never pass
And then was gone, so quickly spent?

Can you recall loves fleeting hour
When with your soul you'd buy delay
Yet couldn't hold the shifting sand
Which with your lover sped away?

Can time exist when happy hearts
Can never hold the moment still
Yet waiting for relief from pain
It's age on age until - until?

Is life then just a walk along
A lane with turnings either way
And at the end when looking back
Was it a life-time or a day?

MY FATHER PLAYED JOANNA.

Playing cops in the jalopy, we would hear
The music swell
Every time the swing doors opened, sounded grand.
There was me and my big brother, with some fizz
And crisps as well,
While my father played joanna in the band.

It's a jewel locked in my memory of a time
Before the war,
In a car beside a pub, allowed up late.
Well, we couldn't go inside, it's a dream
We never saw,
For they don't let kids in pubs down Forest Gate.

I remember scratchy trousers, shirt collars
Far too tight.
"You can sit there till you rot, or eat your greens!"
Cor, my mum she was a handful, she really
Loved a fight
And her world was one of loss and might have beens.

"Son, this life is for the living, grasp it all
And take a chance."
Too young then maybe, but now I understand.
For he'd known the battle trenches and he'd left
His youth in France.
And at night he played joanna in the band.

2

This is a glowing memory of growing up in the 1930's between the two great wars. Possibly an introduction to a misspent youth!

WE GREW UP IN 1940.

We had been evacuated to Suffolk at the outbreak of war. Dad was working at the Arsenal and each time he made the coach trip to see us we begged him to let us come home. My brother Ron was eleven years old now and he said that he was sick of being treated like a farm hand and fed up with looking after me. Hitler didn't seem keen to invade England and many of the evacuees had gone back to London. Dad finally gave in and we returned to a new home in Kent in time for my eighth birthday. After Dunkirk the war became more exciting.

That glorious summer we scrumped apples from the orchard behind the golf house and lay in long grass watching the twisting vapour trails make patterns in the sky. Occasionally we heard the chatter of machine guns and the battle became an extension of the games we played on the ground.
"Dugga, Dugga, Dugga - Dugga, Dugga, Dugga!"
Guns blazing we ran with arms outstretched, ducking and weaving, taking turns to be a Spitfire or Messerschmitt. Aerial combat was known as dogfighting, the spectacle being either "Super" or "Wizard".

About the time that Biggin Hill was bombed Ron and I were cleaning our bikes in the garden when I looked up to see a parachute come swooping over our roof. The mutilated body of an airman hung lifeless in its shroud and the wind carried him over the hill. We had neither seen nor heard anything to explain his sudden appearance but learned later that he was German, had landed in the marshes near Erith and his body was not found.

The Germans started bombing London. Now streams of planes followed the river heading towards the City. On the third Sunday in September, the battle reached its peak. Again Hitler dispatched his bombers for a devastating raid, clouds of smoke blackened the sky line as Woolwich Arsenal and the docks blazed out of control. Dad told us not to go out and said that we could help him bale out the Anderson Shelter which had mysteriously flooded again. Ronnie was forever trying to invent things and convinced that water would run up hill, he fiddled about with some lengths of rubber hose and a funnel. Meanwhile I made myself more useful by sucking up water with a bicycle pump and squirting it at the line of clothes that hung in next door's garden!

Dad rolled up his trousers and lowered himself gingerly into the shelter. The water slopped above his knees and he set to work with buckets, passing them out for us to empty. It may be that we didn't discharge them far enough away, but whatever the reason the water level remained constant. After a spate of furious baling he slung a bucket down the garden and clambered out of the shelter.

"Sod that for a game of soldiers!" he said. I asked him if it had been like that in the trenches but he didn't want to talk about the Great War. Struggling to light a damp cigarette he stomped off into the house.
"He's a bit tetchy" muttered Ron.

That afternoon the bombers came back, wave after wave, we had never seen so many planes before. Dad hustled us into the porch. "Can they see us?" I asked him but he gave no answer, just squeezed me until it hurt. "They look like bloody locusts!" he said. Harried by our fighters the enemy planes throbbed on towards the Capital. Eventually a stricken Dornier broke formation and appeared overhead furiously pursued by a spitting Hurricane. Coughing and spluttering the bomber went into a dive and crashed behind the golf house. A huge cloud of smoke rose from above the woods as the Hurricane executed its victory roll.

Looking down on the links we saw a group of men run into the trees. Knowing they would be getting all the best stuff, Ron and I dashed for our bikes intent on scavenging some souvenirs to add to the accumulating pile of relics we had hidden under our beds. Most prized was a section of a machine gun belt and two live cannon shells. Dad caught us by our collars "You stay here!" he ordered "There are men dying out there!" Fuming beneath his grip we listened to the crackle of exploding ammunition followed by a dull resonating thud as the bomb load exploded.

To the right of the golf house, like tall sentries, three fir trees touched the sky. Each tree was missing the scratchy knot of needle leaves that had crowned its topmost point.

Next day George and I endeavoured to get a better view of the crash site and I challenged him to climb the three pines. I watched his progress with inward glee. I knew that he wouldn't reach the peak of this his first tree and in any case the record was mine for in my pocket were three spiky pine leaves.

It's easy to climb a mature fir if you can reach the first branch, beyond that it's like scaling a ladder. The height that you reach will depend on your weight for the tree narrows to a flimsy spire. As you near the top, the trunk will begin to bend alarmingly, inch a little further and you will find yourself lying almost horizontal watching the ground spin some forty feet beneath you. Master your fear and stretch out your hand to grasp the last piece of foliage. The stem, swaying in protest, will arch downward and blood will rush to your head. If you are small, as I was, you may squirm your way back and the tree will straighten. If you are fat like George the top may snap.

He was now halfway up the first tree.
"Can you see the bomber?" I shouted from the ground.
"Yes" he answered "But I think I'm stuck!"
Clutching my stomach I rolled around on the grass. It was all too perfect!
"Get me down" he called and then a minute later "There's something here."
"Let me look! - What is it George?"
"It's a glove" he said "An airman's glove"
"Throw it down" I ordered and jumped up and down with excitement.
"Shan't" he said and slithered to the lowest branch.
"Oh come on George, bring it down"
"It's mine" he shouted and sitting astride the bough he placed his hand inside the glove.
"Come on George, show me." I was pleading with him now but he didn't seem to notice. His face took on a peculiar green hue and he dropped head first out of the tree. I thought he had broken his neck and my heart thumped as I rolled him over to face me.

6

"George, George, are you alright?"

He opened his eyes and moaned "I think so, what happened?"

"Oh don't muck about" I said and snatched the glove from his hand. Black leather and fleecy lined it was a super airman's glove. I thrust my hand inside but met with an obstruction. Part of a hand was still wearing it!

Subdued now, we pushed the gory relic onto the end of a stick and with an air of solemnity presented it to the soldier who stood guard by the wreckage of the Dornier.

Things had changed, war was real, like a fall from a tree.

POSTSCRIPT

Barnehurst is situated on high ground above the Thames at Erith, eight miles from the London Docks and only a few minutes flying time from Biggin Hill. It provided a perfect vantage point from which to view some of the action later to be known as the Battle of Britain.

The conflict reached its peak on Sunday 15th. September 1940 when the Germans launched massive daylight raids on London. Sixty one Luftwaffe planes were shot down against a loss of twenty six R.A.F. fighters One of the German bombers downed was a Dornier 17 based at Antwerp. Engaged by a Hurricane it crashed behind 'Mayplace' a three storied manor which housed the Barnehurst Golf Club. Three airmen were killed and one taken prisoner.

A crowd of onlookers gathered at the site and disregarding the danger of detonating ammunition attempted to obtain souvenirs. Suddenly the bomb load exploded killing a special constable and three civilians and injuring many others.

"Mayplace" sustained serious damage and eventually the upper floors had to be demolished.

A short distance away a man and three boys were killed by a bomb which was probably jettisoned by the same aircraft. The final casualty figures totalled eleven dead and seven seriously injured.

FEAR

Fear can be delicious, without it there is no secret, challenge or thrill.
Fear makes the heart pump, the body glow, life happen.
Children scream as its fingers approach yet tingle in its grip as they climb
the slide or venture with you to the word of hobgoblins.
Fear is living alert.
Watch though the eyes glaze, body freeze, senses fail, that is terror.
Terror is life distorted, escape routes blocked, tyranny of the soul, the road
to dread.
Dread, timeless nothing, where life has no value, dread embraces oblivion.
Cry for those who enter dread, they are beyond your reach.
Fight for them in terror's grasp, throw them hope.
But envy all those whose broth of life is sprinkled with the herb of fear,
They will know the ecstasy of coming down, regaining breath, of opening
doors.
Try it yourself, peep over the bedclothes to see if the ghost has gone.

****

WISHFUL THINKING.

If I could bring you pleasure
For one moment of your day,
Just one second of enjoyment
That would send the clouds away,
Then I'd know time wasn't wasted
Even though you might forget,
I will hold that treasured memory
Part of life without regret.

GENIUS.

Don't bother me dear while I'm thinking,
I've hung 'Don't disturb' on the door.
Leave the tea on the table
And if you feel able
Clear the plates that you left there before.

I am trying to put it quite plainly.
Listen hard, you might pick up a clue.
While I'm concentrating
Or just meditating
I need time on my own, without you.

How could Einstein have worked out his theories
Being nagged at from morning till night?
Before I get tottery,
I'm beating the lottery
Stoke the fire, 'cos those scratch cards won't light.

I'm aware that the wallpaper's peeling.
Through the roof catch a glimpse of the sky.
Yes, the loo pan is fractured
But I am enraptured
I can find the lost chord if I try.

All mankind will pay me their homage
And history will echo my name
When my works of art
Which I'm going to start
Are hanging in 'Tate' in a frame.

My great saga is just round the corner,
Words will tumble so pure from my brain.
Tell the kids I'm inspired,
It's no wonder I'm tired
Are you working the night shift again?

9

NIGHT RAID.

"C'mon boys, quickly now, bring your blankets."
Dragging us, protesting, from the bed, Dad led us into the hallway.
"Into the cupboard boys and keep your heads down, I'll do a recce to see what Jerry's up to"

As usual the shelter was flooded so our refuge was under the stairs. Father put on his tin hat which rendered him bomb proof and went out to stand in the porch. My twelve year old brother and I huddled together, cold and resentful, bleary eyed through lack of sleep.

As the sirens wailed to a halt we heard the guns start up down river followed by the unmistakable sound of German aircraft. Soon the house throbbed to the erratic beat of their engines.

"Struth, there must be thousands of them" said Ron "Stay here, I'm going to have a decko."
He slipped away and fearful of being alone and bursting with curiosity, I followed him.

The second wave of bombers were right overhead now and the ground trembled as a stick of high explosives screamed down on Erith. Searchlight beams cut the night into slices and the crack of anti-aircraft guns rose to a crescendo. Shrapnel from exploding shells clattered and slithered down the roofs and ten miles up river a red pulsating glow lit the sky like an angry sunset.

We expected Dad to order us back but sensing our need he put reassuring hands on our shoulders. Shielded by his confidence we witnessed night turn into day as Jerry dropped flares which hung in the sky revealing our position. We were exposed, every pilot knew we were there and every bomb aimer was aligning his sights onto our house, but nothing could frighten my Dad. I tugged on his sleeve.

"Was it like this in the last war, Dad, in France?"
"Something like this." he said.
"How long were you in the trenches Dad?"
"Two years off and on."
"You were a crack sniper, weren't you Dad?"
"That's right son!"
The ground convulsed as two bombs screamed down and we heard the sound of breaking glass.
"Keep behind me boys!"
"Struth, that was close." gasped Ron.
Dad tightened his grip on my shoulder.
"You never hear the one that hits you, do you Dad?"

"No never."

"It has to have your number on it, don't it?"

"That's right."

"You went into 'No Man's Land' and got into a crater with your telephone and directed our guns onto the target."

"Yes, I did that a couple of times."

"And you went over the top before the attack and put Bangalore torpedoes under their barbed wire and blew it up."

"Er hmmmm."

"I bet it was muddy."

The sound of the planes had receded, by now they would be over the docks.

"London's copping it again." said Dad

"In the last lot, did you kill any Germans Dad?"

He paused and I looked up to make sure that he had heard me.

"I like to think I didn't son," he said.

Fifty years after the end of the second world war the country was swept by a wave of nostalgia. As a result the media was awash with reminiscences of war and victories in Europe and Japan. Watching these scenes on a Japanese television set seemed to have a touch of irony and prompted the following lines:-

NOW AND THEN.

We switched on our Toshiba and with Riesling in the glass
Sent the kids off to the country, watched the tanks and bombers pass.
And we saw again the places with the names we all recall
Like Rotterdam and Warsaw, Singapore, we watched them fall.

With the places go the faces of the leaders of that time,
Raging speeches urging onward, this from men well past their prime.
They were answered by the young ones in the crushing maws of war,
While the smoke rose out of Auschwitz and the cities were laid raw.

So we stumbled with our prams to escape the burning hell
Or we floundered in the oil on a cold Atlantic swell.
Then we danced along the Strand, we had won and feeling fine,
Turned again to coloured brochures and those cruises on the Rhine.

A MOMENT OF KNOWING.

Clutching his bucket and spade, the naked toddler wobbled towards the sea.

Where dry soft sand gave way to firm wetness he stopped, bewildered, staring at the rivulets left by a receding tide, fascinated by the moisture seeping between his toes.

For the first time he felt alone and as he raised his head his mind absorbed the immensity of space.

For one brief fraction of time he understood his place in the universe. He knew who he was and why he was there. Knew too, that though he might live his full span it would be but a millisecond. He looked at his footprints on the beach and saw that they would wash away just as his existence would wash away. He was between tides.

He moved his feet, saw the sand re-form and understood.

It was implanted, knowledge to be retained until his own tide ebbed.

The moment passed, wonderment gave way to fear.

He turned and with his arms outstretched stumbled back towards his laughing mother.

He piddled as he ran.

****

THE PROMISE.

I shall rise above my body free
Survey the mortal form of me
And move in realms of ecstasy,
In God's good time, so shall it be.

And all the friends that passed before
Will greet with love and what is more,
I'll walk with them on that great shore.
Life is eternal, death a door.

DRY ROT.

Though Uncle Ted has gone his memory lingers.
The only one of us who had green fingers.
Each patch of naked earth
Just had to prove its worth
With manglewurzels, pinks and gay syringas.

The brickwork of his house was made unsightly
By a black strip. one foot up, protruding slightly.
So he covered it with sod,
Planted shrubs and golden rod,
Using bags of steaming dung, he thought quite rightly.

Each year that passed his labour was rewarded,
His friends and all his neighbours, they applauded.
But underneath the floors
Grew a host of fungus spores
Causing damage that he could have ill afforded.

Aunt Else in fishnet tights and red suspenders,
Settled down with gin at hand to watch East Enders.
Uncle Ted was in the kitchen
Unaware of creeping lichen,
Mixing weed and pest control with Auntie's blenders.

Did he have the time to recognise his blunder?
As the ground creaked, groaned then split asunder.
Did he note the frightful error
As he gave a wail of terror?
Did he think of Auntie Else or floribunda?

It was never said of Ted he was a looker,
He was worse when struck by sink and then the cooker.
Auntie Else was quite bereft,
She just packed her bag and left.
They say she works in Soho as a hooker.

The Coroner delivered an oration.
He said that Ted had suffered infestation.
His damp course of existence
Was a line of least resistance
And claimed that Ted had sunk without foundation.

Weeds now thrive and hide the evidence,
Where once roses grew around their residence.
He did not foresee the danger,
He was just a flower arranger,
Poor Uncle Ted's come uppance - subsidence.

SEDUCTION.

RAMBLE

GAMBOL

PECK

NECK

FUMBLE

MUMBLE

SIGH

THIGH

SNAP

SLAP

DISSENT

RELENT

MOAN

GROAN

RAPTURE

CAPTURE.

SUPPLEMENTARY BENEFIT.

I'm not at my best 'til the sun's in the west
And my chin bares it's five o'clock stubble.
The bulk of the day is a limbo of grey
And the morning's a mountain of rubble.

But back at the nest it's comfort and rest
And I'll start with a shower or a dip
Then I'm massaged by Flo, she's a redhead you know
While Nanette brings me whisky to sip.

Next comes barbecued steak or a trout from the lake
Depending on who's at the range, if it's sweet
Suzy Wong, well she hails from Saigon
So it's beanstalks and other things strange.

And so to the dance, be it belly by Blanche
Or flamenco with, what's that broad's name?
I might fancy a movie be it sad, blue or groovy
Or maybe we'll just play a game.

Then the night time will follow, on water bed wallow
We can love 'til all fantasies gone.
But the mornings are hell and I'm not at all well
Yet I must get up now and sign on!

The Ushant lighthouse off the Brittany coast marks the entrance to the English Channel. Returning after a six months voyage the sight of its beacon was inclined to induce an atmosphere of euphoria amongst the crew which was known as 'Channel Fever' - everyone went quite mad.

PINCH OF SALT.

I've gone rolling on a freighter
Down the channel to the bay.
With a cargo bound for Santos
That's down Argentina way.
I'd ship out again tomorrow
If me legs they weren't so poor,
But the vessels they are building
They don't look like ships no more.

I've been crashing through the breakers
Of the Great Australian Bight
And I've seen the bridge at Sydney
From the harbour lit at night.
In the reeking bars of Suez
I've been fleeced by many a whore.
Stuff those floating bulk containers!
They don't look like ships no more.

I've sailed there and back to Boston
Like a pond without a swell.
Yet recall a trip to Capetown
Was a month of screaming hell.
Once we struck the rocks off Rio
Thought we'd never reach the shore.
Have you seen those clockwork tankers?
They don't look like ships no more.

Once you've passed the light at Ushant
Then you know you're homeward bound.
Darn your socks and do your dhobie *
Pack a kit bag full and round.
You'll come steaming up the river
Packed with ships from shore to shore
I'm forgetting it's all gone now
They don't look like ships no more.

*Dhobie - seafaring slang for laundering clothes.

INTRODUCTION.

At the end of the second world war, despite the huge losses, Britain still retained a vast merchant fleet. This gave the opportunity for thousands of young hopefuls to earn their living and travel the world. At the age of sixteen, bored with two years delivering milk, I determined to join them. After completion of an eight week course at the Sea Training School, Gravesend in Kent, I was engaged as a trainee steward by the Royal Mail Lines. My first ship was the m.v. "Highland Monarch" which carried passengers and cargo to South America. We returned with beef from the Argentine, a most precious commodity to those at home still rationed and enduring strict austerity. Each member of the crew was allowed to bring back a personal food parcel - a much coveted bonus.

After completing three trips, I was one of eight boy ratings selected to join the Company's new flag ship nearing completion in Belfast. Travelling by train and then ferry from Hollyhead, we arrived at the shipyard only to find that our cabin in the forepeak consisted of a chalk mark on the deck. Until our accommodation was ready we were lodged ashore.

Built by Harland & Wolff at a cost of nearly £2 million the s.s. "Magdalena" was launched on the 11th. May 1948. In addition to cargo held in three refrigerated holds, she would carry 529 passengers and a crew of 241. Twin screws gave her an average speed of 18 knots. The builders incorporated many new innovations including the biggest attempt ever made to air condition all passenger accommodation and public rooms. After completion and trials she commenced her maiden voyage from London on the 9th. March 1949.

We were thrilled to be part of this new enterprise. It was exciting to watch the ship receive her finishing touches and to take her out on trials. Until hand over to the owners she was known by her builder's number. Each day that we entered the shipyard I saw the number and added its digits together. The others laughed when I voiced my superstitions but we would all remember them later.
The number was 1354.

THE VOYAGE OF THE RMS. "MAGDALENA".

By the inadequate light of my bunk lamp I had read long into the night. At 05.00 hrs. I was in a fitful sleep and involved in a nightmare about the San Francisco earthquake. As the ground shook and the buildings started to tumble I gripped the side rail of my bunk and waited for the tremor to cease. As the dream gave way to reality I became aware that the ship's engines had stopped. Before the alarm sounded I felt again the shaking movement and heard a protesting scream like a stone scraping on slate. One of the lads had been flung from his bed but the others were still asleep. We pulled them roughly out of their bunks and grabbing some clothes and life jackets we made our way to the boat deck. Mustering at our stations we swung the boats outboard and lowered them to the promenade deck. There in the first light of dawn, we could see that we were aground on the Tijucas Rocks, six miles from the coast and fifteen miles away from the spectacular harbour of Rio de Janeiro. The sea was calm. Pale and shaken the passengers appeared in an odd assortment of night clothes and outdoor attire. They helped each other, looking after the children and aiding the frail and elderly. One old lady was disturbed because she hadn't had time to put on her corsets. Many reassured by the apparent lack of urgency returned to their cabins for their valuables or teeth.

Captain Lee had given orders to be called as soon as the pilot boarded. When the ship struck he had dashed to the bridge still in his pyjamas "What the hell are you doing to my ship?" he thundered. His anger was more than justified, bad navigation had placed us well off the correct course for the harbour. While ship's officers conducted a damage survey, passengers boarded the lifeboats where they sat for some three hours.

The vessel was divided into nine compartments by eight transverse water tight bulkheads, with all water tight doors closed we were in no immediate danger. By the slant of the deck it was obvious to all that the ship was well down by the head but only the crew were aware that the forward hold was flooded to the level of the third deck.

The Brazilian navy sent three of her ships to stand by and an assortment of tugs and lighters began to take off the passengers at about 11.00 hrs. Due to the calm sea this operation was completed by noon when the skipper appeared from the bridge to address the crew. I could hardly believe that this haggard figure was the same man I had seen the previous day, he had aged about ten years. He thanked us for our efforts and told us that an attempt would be made to re-float the ship at the next high tide. He gave us the chance to go ashore with the passengers but nobody took up the offer. During the afternoon our situation worsened. Under grey skies the sea began to rise and within an hour we were being pounded by a violent storm. The naval craft and tugs scuttled back to harbour and we were on our own.

Incredibly no pumps had been found on board and as darkness fell it was decided to start a bucket chain. We would attempt to bale out the liner by hand! About fifty of us ventured forward and descended into the crew's quarters. Here the water was waist deep and we took it in turns to wade in and fill our buckets which were then passed back along the line and emptied over the side. Debris floated around us as the sea gradually filled the cabins and corridors and we heard the wooden bulkheads give way under the inexorable pressure. Our efforts were futile but most of us were gripped by a sense of adventure and laboured frenetically for about four hours.

The storm rose to gale force creating a violent corkscrew motion that lifted the stern and drove us further onto the rocks. In the engine room steam pipes and engines were shaken from their mountings. Steam was closed down and the engineers now provided lighting by the use of diesel generators.

It was obvious to us all that should the liner capsize or break up, the lifeboats would be dashed against the hull or thrown onto the rocks. Shortly before midnight, with the tide at its height we heard a tremendous rendering sound. Scraping and groaning the Magdalena slowly drew astern and drifted off the rocks. As the prow dropped into the sea the water level in our corridor rose alarmingly and there followed a mad scramble for the stairs as we abandoned our efforts and raced for the safety of the deck. Once more afloat the anchors were lowered. They held us fast like a duck with its tail in the air.

Throughout the night the stricken vessel withstood a tremendous buffeting. Exhausted by the day's events we snatched a few hours sleep on the floor of the first class lounge. By morning the storm had abated giving way to vast rollers that surged and swept across the deck. Craft ventured out from the harbour including the welcome sight of four tugs. As lines were secured to the stern, small chartered aeroplanes flew over us in order to obtain pictures for the newspapers. There came a new surge of confidence knowing that we were no longer helpless, something was being done, we were going home.

We heard a rumour that now we were taking in water amidships and a new bucket chain was to be formed Lacking any sign of direction or leadership about six of us, all boy ratings, went down to the storeroom alley beneath the galley. At the foot of the companionway we found the water to be quite shallow but looking down the sloping corridor past the storerooms we could see that it reached halfway up the locked watertight door at the end. Forward of that point we knew the decks were flooded and that only the bulkhead held back the sea.

Under tow the ship was moving now and as there was little we could do we decided to return to the deck. Without warning the ship hit a shelf of rock and came to a halt. I clung to the handrail as the water surged away down the alley, smashed against the door then poured back to sweep us off our feet. I saw the bulkhead bulge and water squirted from around the seal of the watertight door.
Again she struck and now we were floundering in the water, reaching out for each other or trying to reach the stairs. Three times in all the tugs pulled us onto the shelf of the rock that marked the deep water level of the harbour's channel, then the tow lines were cut or parted and the Magdalena was drifting again. Desperate now, we pulled each other up the stairs and thinking that I knew the quickest way to safety I yelled at them to follow me.

Two glass revolving doors formed a partial seal between the galley and the air conditioned dining room. Once through the doors we would be able to make our way up the main staircase, through the lounge and bars and out onto the deck. I rushed for the door on the starboard side and flung myself against it but as hard as I pushed the door wouldn't yield. Now the others had joined me but maybe because the central pivot had twisted the door stuck fast. I was pinned against the glass vane with the others crowding behind me. Looking through the glass, to my utter amazement, I saw the tables begin to disappear. "No!" I shouted, but unaware of the danger those behind me continued trying to rotate the door. In front of me a cavernous hole had opened up in the deck of the saloon. Flattened against the thick glass I had a momentary vision of a piano, carpets and chairs tumbling down from the lounges above us. The dining room was split in half and if the door moved we would fall through the decks into the crevasse below. Now, realising what was happening the lads released their pressure on me and panic stricken we turned to find another means of escape.

Everyone seemed to have gone. The ship seemed deserted as we made our way back through the galley and up the tilted corridors towards the stern. We reached the after deck and climbed external stairs towards the promenade, as we did so we could see that the boats were already being lowered. It was a scene of utter confusion, with some boats full and others containing just a few men. A few of the boats hung at crazy angles and as they reached the water the swell lifted them and swung them against the hull. Some boats were still at deck level and I jumped into one only to find that it was right against the break in the hull. The massive steel plates had parted and as we slid down the ship's side I viewed them almost with an air of detachment. The fear of being left behind gave way to a sense of calm curiosity. The forward end of the ship was now largely under water and as the long rolling waves lifted the after end, the plates were buckling in and out like bellows. With her back broken it seemed as if the ship was trying to rid herself of the stern. I was aware that should the tear extend we would be swept into the ship's interior.

We lowered away but were hit by a wave that lifted and flung us against the ship. The lifeboat's wooden gunwale splintered and then we hung above the trough as the next wave rolled in. Somehow we managed to release the falls and furiously pulled away. After so long fighting to save her it seemed strange to be viewing the ship from a distance. About three hundred yards clear of the wreck we stopped for breath and watched her die.

First she appeared to stretch then daylight could be seen through the central break. Gradually the gap widened as the two sections parted company. The stern end swung slightly showing us her broken stump and the interior of her shattered compartments. Without a list and with her screws clear of the water she bore the air of a tattered, broken and much loved toy. Slowly she drifted away from the sunken fo'c'sle and bridge.

A motorised barge drew alongside us and abandoning the lifeboat we jumped in turns onto her slimy deck. The function of this malodorous craft was to transport sewage out to sea and this caused much comment amongst us! To our horror seven or eight figures now appeared on the deck of the 'Magdalena', they waved frantically and started to clamber up the sloping deck of the stern. Very bravely the Brazilian skipper took us back to rescue our stranded shipmates. Exhausted after a strenuous night these men had been snatching some sleep in the sick bay and third class lounge and awoke to find themselves marooned. Our rescue boat went in underneath the 'Magdalena's' moving stern which towered high above us. We shouted encouragement to our mates as they lowered themselves on ropes and dropped into the water. Most of them sustained rope burns and then swallowed oil as they surfaced. One seaman had purchased a magnificent pale blue sombrero in Buenos Aires and was wearing this as he fell into the sea. We pulled him aboard our stinking barge and as he swung over the rail he looked back wistfully at his prize. "I just don't mucking believe it!" he said. Four hundred tons of oranges had been stored in No. 1 hold and these were now escaping. They were forming themselves into a straggling procession which bobbed alongside the hull. Accompanied by this colourful convoy the blue sombrero was floating away on a cushion of oil.

FINALE.

The death throes of the s.s. "Magdalena" were witnessed by thousands of people who thronged the beaches around Copacabana or climbed the Sugar Loaf Mountain. They saw the ship break and watched as the stern half drifted away and beached in Guanabara Bay. The forepeak settled at an angle of 45° with its mast and bridge still visible, the Brazilian flag still fluttered denoting its next port of call. Washed by the tides it would remain there for some months until blasted out of the channel by the Brazilian Navy.

Several crew members swallowed oil while in the water and four sustained steam burns in the engine room, there were no fatalities. Four passengers were still aboard when she broke and were rescued with the crew. The insurance claim for ship plus cargo totalled nearly £3million, the highest loss sustained by Lloyds since the sinking of the "Titanic".

THE SEA.

Porpoise that play and fish that can fly
Albatross watching your ways from the sky.
They know your secrets and don't wonder why
I only know that you call me.

Sometimes you tease with your promised caress
Draw me towards you, murmuring yes.
Sometimes in anger you try to smother
Can't have me one way, you'll try another.

Tropical nights, that's when you are on heat
Dressed up fluorescent, when shall we meet?
You would enfold me, drawing me deep
First comes the ecstasy then comes the sleep.

Breast rise and cleavage, I'll shun your bed
There lie your suitors empty and dead.
You chose the time and you picked the place
They found the perils of your embrace.

Coy to seduce me, flat calm and mild
I've seen your passion raging and wild,
Fickle your moods like a bitch on the spree
I only know that you call me.

25

These lines were written, with affection, for a very dear friend. She is a lady in the most infuriating sense!

WHAT A SHAME.

What a shame that she's a prude
And is never ever rude
Never swears or acts the least bit impolite.
Always stays so prim and haughty
Wouldn't dream of being naughty
Only reads the books that she herself would write.

What hard luck that she's a prude
Even when she's in the mood
How frustrating that she has to turn away.
It would devastate her image
If she tackled in a scrimmage
Because of that she just declines to play.

How grotesque that she's a prude
Even though she has been wooed
She holds herself forever in reserve,
For you can't have many loves
If you wont take off your gloves
Never deviate or give a little swerve.

How disastrous she's a prude,
Never vulgar, never crude,
I would take her for my own
And that's a fact. But she wouldn't take a chance
And her glance is like a lance,
So to mention it would just be lacking tact.

Oh! How sad that she's a prude
At the risk of being sued
I would say it's ten to one she wears a vest.
If she'd only fly with me
Kick her socks off by the sea
She would quickly get the whole thing off her chest.

What a sin that she's a prude
Yet despite her attitude
I would say she has the promise and potential.
If she only stopped declining
Did a little more reclining
We could strip the problem down to bare essential.

What a shame that she's a prude
Prim and proper, never lewd.
Does she never feel the hunger for seduction?
For her looks can still beguile
And she has a secret smile
Is she waiting for some paramount production?

OLD TIMER.

When firemen gather tales are spun
And they are not devoid of fun.
The grimmer side, not taken lightly
Gets boring when regaled twice nightly.

Our predecessors get the huff
And say they're made of sterner stuff.
Let's not forget the things they saw,
They ate the smoke, went back for more.

Long hours they worked for little pay,
Not like the blighter of today,
Who seem to think that it's their due
To live on more than fire-boot stew.

Yet nothing's changed, when on a shout,
We're running in, they're running out,
And flame still clutches, smoke still kills,
We still perform the same old drills.

Old man with tinted glasses, gazes,
Remembering times he went to blazes.
Forgets like us, he played the clown
Off guard until the bells went down.

Don't worry Dad, we're all the same,
It's still a mucky, dangerous game.
Let's brew some tea, relieve the tension,
Hang up your axe and draw your pension.

Anyone who has suffered the torment of bereavement will understand its mixture of emotions; very often anger is one of them. This is an angry poem. I found it helpful to recite this very loudly whilst stomping around the kitchen banging a saucepan lid. Try it, it might make you feel better for awhile.

JUST ANOTHER DAY.

Another bloody funeral, another open grave.
Another mate gone missing without the time to wave.
Another grieving widow and another broken heart.
Another chore, to press the suit, I wear when friends depart.

Another damned donation to the charity of choice.
Another parson praying "He has gone but let's rejoice!"
Another crematorium, another musty church.
Another 'In memoriam', he's left us in the lurch.

Another one has popped off, another bought the farm.
Another kicked the bucket, who never meant no harm.
Another life hereafter, the best is yet to come.
Another blast of trumpets and another roll of drum.

Another lovely fellow or another reprobate.
Another one remembered, referred to as 'the late'
Another wreath with 'Dad' on, a card that's limp with tears.
Another 'It's so sad' on and 'Thank you for the years'.

Another weeping sister or young children and that's worse.
Another grim pall bearer, picking winners in the hearse.
Another flower strewn courtyard, another rainy day.
Another guard of honour and sobs along the way.

Another day of meetings, "Haven't seen you for awhile."
Another way of greeting with a nod across the aisle.
Another shock reminder that time is running out.
Another time to question what the hell it's all about.

Another hug and handshake another parting kiss.
Another person saying "It's his company I'll miss."
Another "See you after, in the pub across the way."
Another bloody funeral, another bloody day.

I have worked in factories and in the Fire Brigade and a long long time ago I went to sea............and I still can't sleep!

INSOMNIAC.

On tropic nights while porpoise weaved
I've manned the crows nest till relieved
And watched fluorescent fish that fly,
While maverick stars fell down the sky.

I've worked the shifts on lathe and press
And pulled the levers under stress
Emerged to blink at dawn's first light
Safe home before the rush hour fight.

Through empty streets I've cut a dash
And pulled up where the blue lights flash,
Then tugged and heaved at metal raw,
Time won't erase the things I saw.

It's over now, I've got the clock,
The plaque on wall and Chinese wok
But still nocturnal, I'm around
To hear the fox come dustbin bound.

Though some count sheep and others scream
And you might take a pill to dream
I'll read my book and sip my wine
And be content, the night is mine.

I regularly walk along this path - a little track of spoilt countryside.

A PATH THROUGH THE WOODS.

On this cold November morning
Take the short cut nature's way.
Station bound with briefcase swinging
Through a woodland in decay.

Blackbird lurches from the bracken,
Muffled now the traffic roar.
Kick aside the empty glue cans
Remnants of the night before.

Fallen leaves conceal the pathway,
Fungi coats the rotting bough.
Frost awaits the filtered sunlight,
Nettles white look friendly now.

Past the supermarket trolley
And the dog's still steaming pile.
Plastic bags with someone's rubbish,
Why do people act so vile?

Beady eyed the flying squirrel
Lifts my spirits, makes my day.
Rat race calls beyond the clearing
Train doors bang, I'm on my way.

OLD BANGER.

Zodiac, Zodiac, Dream dusty Zodiac,
Fording the miles though the clock has wound back.
Once you were sleek as you raced to the sea
Now you lie dormant, decrepit like me.

Zodiac, Zodiac, oxidised Zodiac,
Fifties the memory road that you tack.
Mobile as Bedouin, birds that were game
Cutting a dash you and I were the same.

Zodiac, Zodiac, two litre Zodiac,
Six pistons seized, your suspension is slack,
Lavish of chrome with upholstery hide
Now you decay at the end of the ride.

Zodiac, Zodiac, asthmatic Zodiac,
Damp in your vitals has made you a hack.
Tappets were pitted and valves were all shot
Smoked up and choking a viscous oil clot.

Zodiac, Zodiac, knackered black Zodiac,
Cry on hard shoulder for bits that you lack.
You were my zenith, the star of my life
Long before children, the mortgage, the wife.

Zodiac, Zodiac walnut dash Zodiac,
Standing forlorn on three wheels and a jack.
Crooked your bonnet and battered your boot,
We're bound for the breakers but don't give a hoot.

NEW YEAR.

When first I felt the warmth of you
As dancers swayed and streamers flew
And crushed together, we both knew
That physical attraction.

You tossed your hair and swung to jive
And laughed so vibrant and alive.
Then willed the minute to arrive,
To move another fraction.

We filled our glasses up with wine
To toast another leap in time
Then holding hands to Auld Lang Syne,
We sang in satisfaction.

Much later as emotion urged
We writhed together, bodies merged
Till spent and free all passion purged
We savoured relaxation.

I see you still, our eyes evade.
The perfumes gone, the memories fade.
But still that night, no doubt, we made
A chemical reaction.

It has always struck me that there is a similarity between the modern day truckers and the seamen of old who fought the elements to bring their cargoes home.

HOVE TO.

Cafe lights gleam like a beacon
Like the wreckers' lamps of old
Drew the ships onto the foreshore
For the treasure in their hold.

Open bridge replaced by windscreen,
Reddened eyes strain through the spray.
Turn the wheel but hold the channel,
Peril lurks for those that stray.

Anchored safely in the lay-by,
Drawn there by the siren call.
Raucous music from the juke box,
Raunchy postcards on the wall.

Sultry heat comes onion flavoured,
One armed bandits ping and chime.
Cluttered tables, dirty ashtrays,
Foot hard down has brought him time.

Duffle coats, blue jeans and sweat shirts,
Calloused hands once knew the sea,
Hard from handling ropes on canvas.
Egg and chips with dark brown tea.

Out beyond the streaming windows,
Wave on wave the breakers pound.
Contra-flow and fog speed warnings
Lie ahead, then homeward bound.

THE HOSPICE VISITOR.

"Stay and talk awhile" she said "Please don't pass me by.
I get so nervous, tell me plain, what is it like to die?
If there's just nothing , I should know.
Tell me the truth before I go."

"First you must understand " he said "about the light. Immune to physical harm, independent of rules and law, unseen except by the gifted few, the body glows with light. Ever-changing, it pulsates without heat, ballooning and diminishing in response to emotion, energised by motive. Eyes can deceive and words can falsify but this radiance is of the inner self. It cannot lie. Glowing with myriad colours according to your moods it is of you, yet separate. The part that matters most, yet is not matter.

Only the body dies and as it weakens so the light intensifies and begins to move away. Soon it has formed above the body, held only by a slim cord. From this time you are in touch with paradise. It will be like going home, for you have been there many times before. The body doesn't matter, you will be glad to be free of it's limitations. We all have our time. You will see other souls waiting to greet you, bathed in a greater light that vibrates with love. It's like going through a door. The last great adventure. That is what it is like to die."

"I haven't always been good" she whispered "Sometimes I've been mean.
I've kept quiet when I should have spoken, shut my eyes to things I've seen."
............"Don't be afraid, there is no devil
Just realms of enlightenment, each finds his level."

"You have to understand" he stressed "about the scales. It is a balance weighed by thought, first tipping one way and then the other. All the good things that you have been and all the love you gave have tipped the scales in your favour. There are levels of light waiting to receive, each soul enters that intensity it has itself created. The soul makes it's own environment and your soul will move in high realms, for you are full of love. It's natural law and very simple, only man has made it confusing. Try to rest now."

"I'm not afraid now" she said "I think I am ready."
Her eyes were alert and her voice was steady.
"You are so confident, so certain.
As if you have been beyond the curtain."

"I have this on the very best authority" he said "I'll see you again tomorrow.".
"I may not be here" she replied.
"I know" he said softly.

ROSIE.

What can I say about Rosie
That hasn't already been said?
How can I tell her I like what I see
And I see what I like in my head?

When Rosie retires to her bedroom
In nightie, with cocoa and book
This long distance lover, peeps under the cover
Though five miles away, I still look!!

If you think that I'm going to tell you who Rosie is you're mistaken.
Find your own fantasy!

THE HELLEMENTS.

Have you noticed how the nights are drawing in now?
And the leaves have blocked the drains again today?
All the trees look gaunt with fear,
It's too cold for drinking beer.
Can it be that blooming winter's on the way?

As I rummage in the cupboard for my moon boots,
There's a smell of Autumn bonfires in the air.
As if conscious there'll be cuts,
Wiley squirrel saves his nuts,
But I'll put my faith in thermal underwear.

I've got jet lag now the clocks have been retarded,
This time last week it wasn't now at all.
So I've just reset the heating
To provide a warmer greeting
And to dry the mildewed brolly in the hall.

All the seasons have their snags and compensations,
Spring is fine, that's when it comes, which sometimes aint.
And the summer's full of glory
But that's another story
And the Autumn is what painters like to paint.

But the winter strains my wits to give it credit,
Stay in bed, none but a fool would venture out.
Pull the blinds and pass the brandy,
Cuddle up I might get randy,
For survival is what nature's all about.

Having seen how a 'simple little thing' like a children's party had reduced my wife to a gibbering, nervous wreck, I decided to put pen to paper. So as not to be accused of chauvinism it is written from a woman's view point.

THE PARTY.

Clutching presents, eager faces
Shiny shoes and tied up laces.
Each one told to watch his manners
Ten potential little spanners.

Guest of honour in Dad's chair
Mark is here and Philip there.
Hands are clean, then you may start
Locust-like the fingers dart.

Cake is lit, nine candles glow
Wish as hard as you can blow.
Promised not to call him little
Flames are dowsed by breath and spittle.

Sandwiches with pickled onions
Cheeks are puffed like facial bunions.
"Happy Birthday" sing and clap
Crisps and fruit juice in each lap.

Second portions need I ask?
Stuffing trifle through face mask.
Open window Paul feels sick
Sense my eye start nervous tic.

Pinching starts and nudges deft.
Lav is first door on your left.
Cake is snatched, it isn't fair.
Who put jelly in Bob's hair?

Turn them out into the garden
Neighbours use of, nerves to harden.
Signal Mayday, children's treat
Sinking fast with swollen feet.

Ted just rang he couldn't make it
Overtime, has got to take it.
Funny that, the Aspirin's mine.
Garden flooded, John is nine.

BOWLED OVER.

Another age, when in my prime,
Before I sensed the hand of time,
I knew a girl with golden hair,
Long shapely legs and figure rare.
In Danson Park I took her strolling
Then paused awhile to watch the bowling.
The players', weighing line and pace,
Despatching woods with languid grace.

Her lilting voice, like waterfalls,
"Why do they have such odd shaped balls?
They bowl them crooked, out and back,
But hardly ever hit the jack."
We found it slow and downright boring
So turned away with passion soaring.
Her virtue hung now by a thread
"It's just an old man's game" I said.

We found a glade concealed from view
And fumbled as young lovers do.
Then later, in her father's shed,
We used rough peat sacks for a bed.
Ensconced within that earthy hovel,
Investigating postures novel,
Were interrupted, caught, undone,
Her nosey mother marred the fun.

With time, it's merely sheer conjecture,
How we survived with just a lecture.
But Mum seemed free of inhibitions
While Dad did night work on munitions.
My leave flew fast, I had to sail,
She said she'd wait, I promised mail.
But teenage love is fast and fleeting,
While Aussie Sheilas take some beating.

40

Through fifty years I nursed that vision,
But now an object of derision,
With shiny head and portly frame,
I've found at last the perfect game.
Now matched against a team unseen,
I set my woods out on the green.
We won the toss, I played as skip,
Proud master of a fated ship.

That dream I'd cherished in my slumber,
Shook hands as my opposing number.
Her voice, those dulcet tones now shattered,
Boomed and grated as she nattered.
The golden hair that once delighted
Was sort of grey with mauve highlighted.
Those legs, once perfect calves and thighs,
Were bowed, recalling 'Bridge of Sighs'.

And yet I knew and so did she,
As teams engaged in repartee.
Her eyes retained that magic lustre,
The "Follow me lads" of General Custer.
"You wont remember me" I stated
And checked my pulse rate while I waited.
Bewitching me with her persona,
She said "You're Mo and I am Mona."

We lost the game, in truth I blew it,
At least I bowled, she almost threw it.
Her woods were fired full strength with verve,
They split the pack and broke my nerve.
At tea break, close, we reminisced,
It dawned on me the chance I'd missed.
So, I recalled her garden shed
"It's not an old man's game" she said.

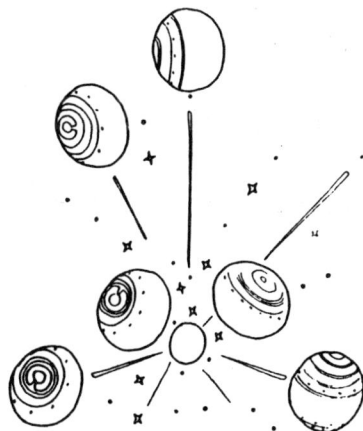

REUNION.

When firemen gather tales are spun
And they are not devoid of fun
The grimmer side not taken lightly
Gets boring when regaled twice nightly.

You have to admit that they are starting to go to seed now. They wander around patting each others beer bellies and saying "What's all this then?" A couple of them use walking sticks and those that aren't bald are grey. They tend to cup a hand to one ear and shout "Come round here and talk, I can't hear a word with all this noise going on."

Most of all they laugh, great guffaws that raise your spirits and make you feel alive and part of an elite band.

These old firemen of every rank meet regularly at a local club and seem to have forgotten what a dirty, dangerous, gruelling job it was. They don't talk of winter nights when the spray from the jets froze on their fire tunics or of the heat that sometimes buckled their knees. They appear not to remember staggering out of jobs, choking, covered in muck or soaked to the skin, eyes streaming and mucous streaming black from their nostrils.

They never speak of groping around in thick smoke trying to search an unfamiliar building and knowing that their breathing apparatus was fast running out of air supply.

They have known the terror of floors caving in and walls collapsing and many have the scars to show for it. These things aren't mentioned They chat about good fire stations, decent guv'nors, right bastards, real characters and departed comrades. The conversation is peppered with nicknames, Dibble, Timber, Muffin, Wally and Ned. The language is colourful and mostly insulting but nobody seems to care.

"You're looking for a job? About time too, you never did any frigging work in the Brigade!"

"Get the bolt cutters, it's Rob's turn to buy a round but his wallet's seized up!!"

Stories are told thick and fast, embellished with each telling.

"We went to a fire in a furniture depository and the ruddy place was smoke logged. Four of us rigged in B.A. * and entered the second floor. Couldn't see a finger up your nose. Well, I found this door and went through and the others crowded in behind me. We were stopped by a wooden wall. We cut our way through and opened another door, it didn't lead anywhere - there was another wall, we knocked it down and found a door. By the time the smoke had cleared we had smashed our way through about twenty wardrobes!"

"What about that old dear who brush painted her bath? It looked so good when she finished that she didn't give the enamel time to dry. When we got there she was stuck fast and it took three of us and a pound of butter to get her out. Even then we left half her bum behind. My eyesight's never been the same since."

"This bloke was kneeling on the kitchen floor laying floor tiles. The fumes from the glue caught alight from the boiler and there was a flash-over. He crawled outside on his hands and knees just as the gas main went and blew his house in half. I came across him in the garden, he was covered in plaster and was minus most of his hair and eyebrows. 'I was trying to surprise the wife!' he said. Well, I had to bite my tongue."

"Do you remember the night of the bad flooding Mo? Back in '69 I think it was. We went down this hill in torrential rain and it was like going over Niagara. Rumble, the Sub-Officer was yelling at Mo to slow down but Mo ignored him! Well, we hit this puddle at the bottom of the hill and it's at least four feet deep. I swear this wave went right over the cab and we were sitting there with water around our knees. Rumble jumped out of the cab, the water was up to his armpits and he was calling Mo all the names under the sun. Mo shouted out 'Abandon Ship' silly arse!"

The air is full of "What's his name?" "What about....." "Who was?" and "Y'know......."
"Who was that Leading Fireman that ran off with the station cook? Y'know, her husband came up the station dead worried because they were using his car. 'I'll never get it back' he said"

Ernie has organised everything and about ten o'clock he indicates he is ready to go home by clearing up the buffet. People begin to move. There's lots of back slapping and "See you next month if your zimmer frame works!" Then they are off into the night, tough old lads, still full of fire.

* B.A. Breathing Apparatus

And for those who sneak a look at the last page,
this is how it ends........

IN

THE BEGINNING.

In the beginning there was just a big hole,
Full of nothing and therefore quite boring,
Like a BBC soap or a year on the dole,
Or lying awake while he's snoring.

Then came a big bang, though what banged, I'm not clear
And bits flew around, 'twas amazing.
And all of a sudden the earth was right here
With fields, trees and dinosaurs grazing.

After billions of years, give or take a few days,
Life was formed from primeval gravy.
Then man came along with his devious ways
With hair on his bum, thick and wavy.

He carried a club as he looked for his mate
He made sounds, sort of grunts, groans and honking.
When he found what he wanted, on very first date
Well he wasted no time but got bonking.

It's not like that now, he's made progress you see,
'Stead of club he just raises his hat.
He no longer howls, from high cliff top or tree,
And I'm rather sad about that.